RESTORIA
HARBOR OF HOPE

MORIAH JOHNSON

SCRIPTOR HOUSE
THE EPITOME OF GREATNESS

Scriptor House LLC
17434 Bellflower Blvd Ste 200-188 Bellflower, CA 90706
www.scriptorhouse.com
Phone: +1209-554-8271

Paperback: 979-8-88692-383-4
eBook: 979-8-88692-392-6

CONTENTS

Reaching Your Goal

It's about a woman who's struggling to reach her goal in life. In spite of the things she has been through in her past and also what she facing in her present. Although sometimes she gets down and weak, she constantly presses until she reaches her goal. She had known loss in ways that most people couldn't begin to imagine. Her childhood was filled with pain—abuse that took root in her heart long before she even understood what it was. She carried the weight of it silently, too afraid to speak, too lost in the darkness to reach out. As she grew older, the wounds from her past followed her like shadows, always just behind her, lurking. Each failure, each setback, felt like another reminder of how unworthy she was, how little she deserved the happiness she once dared to dream about.

But there was something inside of her that refused to break. Even when the world seemed determined to keep her down, even when the people she loved turned their backs or let her down, she kept going. Some days, it was the tiniest thing that kept her from falling apart—an old song that reminded her of better times, a fleeting moment of kindness from a stranger, a whisper in her mind telling her that maybe she could make it after all.

She had learned to fight without anyone showing her how. She was bruised and scarred—inside and out—but those scars had become a part of her strength. She didn't know how to be gentle with herself. She didn't know how to stop. Because giving up meant giving in to the very things that had broken her. And she wouldn't do that.

There were days when the exhaustion was unbearable, when the weight of her own history threatened to crush her under its pressure. She would lie awake at night, haunted by memories of abuse and loss, wondering if she'd ever be free. But in the quiet of those moments, she would dig deep, finding a flicker of courage. A belief that maybe—just maybe—there was more to her life than what she had been through.

With each small victory, she grew stronger, but the road was never easy. She stumbled, she fell, and sometimes she didn't know how she'd keep going. But she kept pressing on, because she knew what the alternative was—letting her past define her forever. And she wasn't willing to let that happen.

She didn't know what "success" looked like, but she knew it wasn't about the thing's others had, the validation or applause they received. It was about finding peace, finding herself, and knowing, deep down, that she was worthy of a life that was hers to claim.

And one day, when she finally reached that goal—whatever it was—she would realize that the true victory wasn't in the destination. It was in the courage it took to keep walking when every part of her wanted to give up. It was in surviving, in fighting, in reclaiming herself from the darkness. And in the end, she'd learned something far more powerful than how to reach her goal: how to keep going, no matter what.

CHAPTER 1
GROWING UP (CHILDHOOD LIFE)

Growing up as a little girl was not easy. We were a family of eight, four sisters and four brothers. I was the oldest girl in the family, but have a brother who is older than me. We were from the North Side of Chicago, where we stayed in a one-bedroom apartment. At that time I was five years old, Kathy and William fought a lot. All I could remember was William coming home from jail the next morning. I would get out of bed and go in the living room and he would be there. At my age, I was a very mature girl. I loved to wash dishes and also help William cook at times. He was a great chef. I and my siblings would destroy the house on many occasions. One day we came home from school, we wet the couch with buckets of water this was really fun. My sister Alicia and brother Craig got in trouble, but not me. They would always ask why I didn't not get in trouble. I knew the reason why but was afraid what people would say.

One night all of us were getting ready for bed, we had bunk- beds that we slept in. My oldest brother David and younger brother Craig slept in the bottom bunk. I and Alicia slept in the top bunk. That same night William came in the room and woke me up. He told me to come with him. I did what I was told because I trusted and really loved this man. So, he took me in the room and began to talk to me and he told me to take off my clothes. At that time, I was only five years old and did not know what was going on, therefore I did what I was told. He grabbed the Vaseline and rubbed it between my legs and also on his private part. I did not know what to expect, suddenly there was a knock at the door. He told me to hold on, it and it was someone for Kathy, however she was not there. He came back in the room and began to molest me, afterwards he sent me back to bed. It was crazy because my brother David was not sleep and he knew everything that happened. Kathy did not come home until the next morning and my brother David tried to tell her what happen but she said he was lying. Kathy told my brother David that something like this would never happen he must be mistaken.

After that, the situation was never spoken of again. But things quickly began to unravel for the family. Kathy and William separated, and we moved to the West Side of Chicago, seeking some kind of escape, but the reality we walked into was far worse than we could have imagined. When we moved, everyone ended up at Flora's house. Kathy's siblings, their kids—all of us crowded into that small space. It wasn't much of a home. It wasn't a safe place. In fact, it was a nightmare.

The house was haunted. Not the kind of haunted where you hear a door creak or see a shadow in the corner of your eye. No. This place was crawling with evil spirits. There was something wrong in that house, something that made the air thick and suffocating. As kids, we couldn't shake the feeling that something was watching us, something dark and malicious. We didn't feel safe there—not with the spirits, and certainly not with some of our own family members.

The truth is, we were all being molested. Kathy and her sister were never around to protect us, leaving us to fend for ourselves in a house that wasn't really a home. No one cared enough to check on us, to see what was happening behind closed doors. We were left to navigate the world on our own, without guidance, without protection.

Our parents were ghosts in our lives, often disappearing for days, sometimes weeks at a time. It felt like they didn't even notice we were starving, that we were struggling to survive. We didn't even have the luxury of being kids. We were forced to grow up too fast, too soon. Our only hope for food was the apple tree in the front yard. When there was nothing else, we'd pick apples— sometimes just to fill the aching emptiness inside us, sometimes to keep from feeling completely invisible.

My brother David was the only one trying to hold things together. He worked at a barber shop down the street, and when he got paid, he'd bring us food—if he could. Our meals? Ramen noodles. Every. Single. Day. We were sick of it, but it was all David could afford. It was all we had.

And when there was nothing left to eat, when hunger gnawed at us like a constant companion, we resorted to stealing. Desperate, ashamed, but driven by an insatiable need to survive. I remember that coat. It was a long, tattered thing, full of holes, barely holding together. Me, my sister Alicia, and my brother Craig would take turns wearing it, huddling into it like it could protect us from the world. But nothing could protect us. Not from the hunger, not from the loneliness, and certainly not from the things we had to do just to stay alive.

One day, it was Alicia's turn to steal. We'd done it countless times before, but this time was different. This time, we were caught. We had never been caught before, but on that day, the gas station clerk saw her. He grabbed her, and in that instant, the illusion of control shattered. My brother Craig and I ran. We didn't look back. We couldn't. The fear was suffocating, and the panic pushed us forward, but we knew—nothing was ever going to be the same again.

It was funny to us as kids, in a twisted sort of way, but Alicia was crying—just like always. The man in the store could have called the police. He could have had us arrested, but he didn't. He let us go. Looking back now, I can only say, *Thank you, Jesus,* because we could've ended up in jail. But we didn't.

I tell people all the time: when you're desperate, you'll do things you never thought you would. And that's what we did. Was it right? No. But we had to eat, and that's how we ate. We didn't have choices. Just survival.

Soon enough, it was time to move again. The house we were staying in had burned down, and just like that, we were separated once more. My two brothers, Julian and Craig, went to live with Aunt Joyce. I moved in with my best friend, whose sister was my godmother. My other sisters stayed with Flora. The separation hit me harder than I can even explain. Being torn apart from my siblings, knowing we were going to different homes—it hurt in ways I can't put into words.

There were days when I didn't eat at all. No food. Nothing. My friend's mom didn't have gas, so we were freezing in that cold apartment. I was out of school because no one bothered to enroll me. Sometimes, I slept on the streets, not knowing where my next meal would come from. Me and my friend would walk from the West Side to the North Side, trying to hustle, trying to find any way to make money. We were just kids, but we had to survive.

Eventually, my godmother couldn't take care of me anymore. She sent me back to Kathy, who was spiraling deeper into her drug addiction. She didn't have time for us—didn't have the energy to care. We bounced from shelter to shelter, never staying in one place for long. Going to school was no longer even an option—it became normal to not go.

I felt like Kathy had already given up on us. She'd sent my brothers away, and it seemed like she didn't want to deal with us anymore. Our family was unraveling. Flora was struggling to take care of her own kids and grandkids, and Kathy's decision to send us to William felt like our last hope. I was in six grade when we moved in with William and his girlfriend, Brenda.

That's when we found out we had a brother on our dad's side. His name was Kenon, and he was just four months old. Suddenly, as the Big Sister, I didn't know how to feel about it.

We lived in a tiny studio apartment for over a year. There was barely enough space for the four of us, let alone the five of us with a baby now. We slept on the floor. William and Brenda squeezed onto a pull-out couch. We were all cramped in that tiny, cold space, trying to make the best of it, but it was suffocating. Eventually, they moved us to a bigger apartment, but the struggles didn't end. William would blow the money on drugs, and we'd be left with nothing. Bills piled up. Food was scarce.

I became the one who had to take care of us. I cooked every meal for me and my sisters. Brenda would eat her food raw, so that left me with the responsibility of feeding us. I had to comb all of our hair, get us ready for school every day, all while trying to keep it together myself.

But things didn't get better. They only got worse. William's behavior—his constant advances toward me—grew more frequent, more aggressive. I was terrified. Terrified to speak up because when my brother David had told Kathy what was happening, she didn't believe him. She dismissed him, like his words didn't matter. So I stayed silent.

This went on for months—six months of my life that I can't get back. I hated the way I was touched, but I didn't know how to stop it. The fear kept me quiet, kept me paralyzed in a way I didn't even understand.

Then, when school was about to start again, something shifted. My dad was doing better—he'd managed to pull himself together. He took us shopping for clothes and school supplies, something I never thought would happen. It was the first time in a long while I felt something resembling hope. William even took us to the beauty shop, the first time we'd been there in forever. We were excited, maybe for the first time in a long time, feeling like we might get a chance at something better.

But in the back of my mind, I knew things were still fragile. Still unpredictable. But at least, for a brief moment, there was something to look forward to.

We all knew that our first day of school that year was going to be different from the others. The excitement of starting fresh made us hopeful that things could get better. School began that following Monday, and our original plan was to go grocery shopping to get some essentials. But things took a sudden turn when William disappeared—and he didn't come back. It became a recurring pattern that we couldn't ignore. His absence was becoming the norm, and with every disappearance, things only got worse.

William's girlfriend, Brenda, was furious with him, and instead of directing her anger at him, she took it out on us. She made our lives unbearable. For days, she refused to feed us, leaving us hungry and helpless. Worse still, she abandoned us at home alone, forcing my younger sisters to cry in hunger and fear. My heart broke for them, but I couldn't afford the luxury of crying. I had to be strong for them. I had to protect them, no matter what. So, I promised myself that no matter how difficult things got, I would take care of my sisters and make sure they were safe.

After two unbearable days, Brenda came back. She told us to get dressed and then drove us to my Auntie Joyce's house, where my two brothers were already staying. It was strange—she dropped us off and left, like she had never been part of our lives. But she made one mistake: she left her food stamps with me. The moment she was gone, I knew I had to take action. Brenda had been so cruel to us, and I couldn't let her get away with it. So, I lied. When she came back to collect the food stamps, I told her I had lost them. I knew it wasn't the kindest thing to do, but after all the hurt she had caused, I felt justified.

I handed the food stamps to Auntie Joyce, believing she would use them to buy us some food. Auntie Joyce had always been known for her kindness—she had already taken in my brothers, and I thought she would do the same for us. She was the type of woman who opened her home to anyone in need, taking care of other people's children as if they were her own. It seemed like a blessing that we were going to stay with her.

The apartment we moved into was small—a cramped three-bedroom with barely enough space for everyone. Auntie Joyce already had her two daughters living there, along with another niece she had taken in. It was crowded, and everything felt chaotic. There was barely any room for us, but we made do. We squeezed in, trying to find a place for ourselves in this overstuffed space. Her boyfriend was there too, at first seeming nice and friendly, but that didn't last long. His attitude shifted, and it didn't take long for things to feel uncomfortable.

Every morning, my siblings and I would clean the house. We were always told to clean. We cleaned walls, we cleaned rooms, and we cleaned every inch of the house. Auntie Joyce and her children weren't exactly the cleanest people, and though I wasn't thrilled about doing all the work, they seemed to appreciate how well I did it. But that appreciation didn't last long. Soon, it became expected of me. They saw the potential I had, and they began to take advantage of it. My siblings and I were treated like house slaves, forced to clean up after everyone without much recognition. We had to do the chores while Auntie Joyce's daughters lounged around, telling us what to do, never lifting a finger to help.

Her youngest daughter, just a year younger than me, was spoiled. As the baby of the family, everyone treated her like royalty. It was maddening. She barely had to do anything, and the more she was babied, the more frustrated I became. Here I was, doing everything I could to make sure my siblings were taken care of, while this girl barely had to lift a finger. The favoritism was so blatant that it made my skin crawl.

Eventually, Auntie Joyce registered us in school. That was a huge struggle in itself. Since we had been out of school for so long, there were no records for us, and it felt like they might fail me just because I was behind. The school was across the street, and luckily, since her children went there, the staff was willing to work with her. After much persistence, I was enrolled in seventh grade, but I still worried that they would hold me back. It had been a long time since I'd been in school, but thankfully, they placed me in my proper grade.

Catching up was no easy task. It was hard at first, and my Iowa test scores were embarrassingly low, but the teachers were kind. They worked with me day after day, helping me understand the concepts again, and little by little, I started to grasp everything. I knew that I couldn't fall behind—I had to keep going for my siblings, for myself. Despite the hurdles, I pushed myself, staying up late and working as hard as I could.

My sisters were enrolled in school alongside me, and my brothers were already there, so at least we had each other. Slowly, things began to settle. We moved again, this time to a larger, four-bedroom apartment across the street. I thought this new space would bring relief, but I was wrong. It only got worse.

By then, we hadn't seen our parents in over a year. Auntie Joyce had become overwhelmed, and she told us she couldn't afford to keep taking care of us. That's when she called DCFS (Department of Children and Family Services). We begged her not to send us away. We didn't want to be split up again. We told her we wanted to stay with her, and DCFS, after hearing us out, allowed us to stay. But the agency's involvement meant we were now part of the system.

It was a bittersweet victory—yes, we could stay, but now we were tied to the state, dependent on monthly checks that were supposed to help us survive.

DCFS also provided us with clothing and bed vouchers, which seemed like a small consolation. Auntie Joyce took us shopping with the vouchers, but when we got to the store, something devastating happened. She didn't buy anything for my sister Alicia. She spent all the money on her own daughters. Alicia was left empty-handed, and it broke my heart to see her so sad and hurt. She was the only one who didn't get anything to wear, and she cried for days afterward. Auntie Joyce promised her she'd take her shopping again, but that promise was never kept. It wasn't surprising, though. In a house full of selfishness and neglect, we should've expected that. It was so sad and depressing because she was getting the big bucks us at least two thousand dollars a month.

It was finally time for me to graduate from grammar school, and I was over the moon with excitement. I had made it further than anyone ever thought I would, especially after all the obstacles I'd faced. So many people had doubted me—people who said I wouldn't make it, that I'd end up like Kathy, stuck in a cycle with no way out, having a bunch of kids and doing nothing with my life. But here I was, about to graduate. It felt like a victory for me and my siblings, a moment that proved everyone wrong.

It was the summer of 1993, and the city was still buzzing with excitement after the Chicago Bulls had just won their championship. The energy was contagious, everyone on the streets celebrating, and for the first time in a long time, it felt like something good was happening—not just in my life, but in the world around me.

The night before my graduation, Kathy came by to see me, and it made me so happy. It had been a while since we'd spent time together, and I had missed her presence. She was always so full of life, and I thought she believed in me.

That same night, Kathy took me to her house, and we spent hours doing my hair and nails although I wanted to go to the beauty shop. However, It was one of those rare moments where I could just be a teenage girl, doing something normal and fun, without worrying about all the responsibilities weighing me down. It felt like a small act of love, and in that moment, I felt special.

The next morning, we arrived back at my house, and everything was set for the big day. I remember feeling a mix of nerves and excitement, but mostly, I just felt proud of how far I had come. I was about to walk across that stage, a moment I had worked so hard for, despite everything that had tried to hold me back. The people who doubted me, who thought I wouldn't make it—well, they were about to see me prove them wrong. I was already down in spirit because I wanted to go to the beauty shop and get my hair and nails done. I had worked so hard to get to this point—graduating from grammar school— and it felt like I deserved something more, something better than what I had been given. I had always been told that I wasn't going to make it, that I would end up like Kathy—having kids young and doing nothing with my life. But here I was, about to graduate, and I was proud of myself for defying the odds. The people around me didn't always see my struggle, and I couldn't help but feel bitter about the lack of recognition. The money that DCFS was giving for us—why couldn't I have something of my own? I worked for this, so why couldn't I get something as simple as a new dress for my graduation?

Instead, I wore an old polka dot dress that the pastor's daughter had given me. I appreciated it, but it wasn't what I had hoped for. I'd worked so hard to graduate, and I thought I deserved better than this—something new, something that felt like a reward for all the effort I had put in. But still, I showed up in that dress, ready to walk across that stage and prove I was more than what others thought of me.

When it came time for graduation, there were awards for scholarships and monetary prizes, and I had no idea that I would be one of the recipients. I was completely shocked when I heard my name being called. They had two monetary awards to give out, one for the most improved student, and the other was an award from the school. And there I was, standing there, holding one of them. I couldn't believe it. It was a recognition I had earned, and in that moment, it felt like all my hard work and determination had paid off.

After graduation, I couldn't wait to cash the awards. Kathy, who had been so supportive and encouraging throughout the whole process, convinced me to go with her instead of going with my friends. Part of me wanted to be with my friends to celebrate, but Kathy's insistence led me to agree. We went over to my Auntie Tory's house—my mom's sister. Auntie Tory had always been proud of me, especially after everything I had gone through. Out of all my aunts, she was the one who had things together, who had her life in order, and I felt a sense of security when I was with her.

I stayed over there for a while, waiting for Kathy to come back as promised. She had the money I had just received, holding onto it while I waited. I didn't think much of it at first; I trusted Kathy. But when she came back, everything changed. She came back, not with my money, but with nothing. She had spent all of it on drugs. My heart dropped when I realized what had happened, and the tears came rushing out. I cried so hard—angry, hurt, and devastated. I had worked so hard for that money, and now it was gone. She reassured me that she would pay me back, but I didn't know how or when that would happen. All I knew was that she had taken something from me that I couldn't get back.

Kathy left for a bit, but I stayed at my aunt's house, hoping for some comfort, some solution. But instead, we ended up leaving and going to Kathy's house, where I stayed the entire weekend. It wasn't the celebration I had envisioned— it wasn't the reward I had worked for. It was just more of the same. I felt the weight of everything I had been through and how easily things could slip away from me, even when I thought I had a chance at something good.

The weekend came to an end, and Kathy still hadn't managed to come up with any money for me. She brought me back home empty-handed, and the feeling of betrayal weighed heavy in my chest. Not only had she taken something so important from me, but she didn't even seem to care. When I walked through the door, I was greeted by my friends' laughter, and I could feel the sting before they even said anything. "Kathy spent your money on drugs," they mocked. The words felt like a slap in the face. I wanted to sink into the ground, to disappear, but instead, I stood there, holding back tears.

It wasn't just the money. It was everything that had been building up—the disappointment, the feeling of being let down again, and the shame of having something so important taken from me. But that wasn't the only thing that hurt. My heart ached because William—my father—didn't even show up to my graduation. He didn't come to see me walk across that stage, didn't offer any words of encouragement or pride. I had worked so hard to make it to that moment, and I felt like I had no one to share it with.

Yet, in the midst of all that pain, I refused to let it break me. I couldn't. I had come too far, fought too hard to let these things take me down. So, I kept my head up. I pushed the hurt to the back of my mind, swallowed the tears, and stayed strong. It was the only choice I had. No matter how much it hurt, I knew I had to keep going. I had made it this far, and I wasn't going to let anyone or anything pull me back into the darkness.

CHAPTER 2

TEENAGE LIFE

It was the fall of 1993, school was about to begin. I was so excited this was my first year of high school. I wanted to see how it really was. I was excited about going but sad because I did not have any new clothes. My aunt Joyce did not take any of us shopping. Sometimes I could not understand because I was never a child that asks for much, but I did want new clothes to start high school. I started at Metro High School, it was also right across the street from me. Thank God for that because if it was up to my aunt Joyce that we were living with we probably would not have made it to school on some days. So every day I walked to school. On my first day I decided to hang out with my cousin that went there. She was a junior there; this cousin was Kathy sister daughter. When I went it was hard for me to find my classes, as you know high school is bigger than grammar school. They just laugh and said that they must be freshmans. One of my most embarrassing moments was, I went to lunch and sat by my cousin and her friends and she let them talk about me. I was so hurt because she knew I did not have anything and it was not my fault. But I choked it up and kept on stepping. I met other friends from some of my other classes that I was in. I met one girl who turned out to be my best friend in high school. Her name was Lovely she hated that name I thought it was such a beautiful name. Anyhow, we hung together all day every day. We had a lot of classes together but one class I remember the most was gym. In gym while taking swimming the guys used to pull us underneath the water so we stop getting in the water. Our gym teacher called us the "F" crew. However, we made such improvement the next semester, I also met another friend. He ended up being my best guy friend, his name was Robert. When you saw Robert, you saw me that's how cool we were. We were so close people thought we were together as a couple. He also wore my picture around his neck every day. High school now was seemed a little easy since I had friends and we all stuck together. However, I hated to leave school sometimes because I did not want to go home. I hated to go home because we could not do anything at home. The only thing we did was clean up. I did not have to do homework because I always finished that at school. Therefore, I tried to participate in every activity they offered at the school. Another reason why I did not want go home was because a lot of men used to be at our house. Sometimes when I made it home my aunt boyfriend brother would be over there and he would always tell me he wanted to be the first one to have sex with. It scared me because I was already molested by other men in my family, now somebody else comes along and tell me what they want to do. He had a lot of money I guess that's why he thought I would say yes. I never expressed it to anyone because people just did not hear little girls when they said they were being molested. We used to also make our money by going over my aunt daughter house to clean up. Her boyfriend was the guy who ask me to let him be my first. So, every weekend, I and my cousin would go over there and we slept in the guest room. Some night he would come in the room and have me to open my legs and would stick his fingers in me. There would always be chicken bones in the room from the previous night. Till this day I do not like the smell of chicken bones. It makes me think about what he was doing to me. Eventually, I made an excuse to stop going over there; everyone was trying to figure out why I was not going over there anymore. I thought to myself money doesn't mean nothing to me I was tired of being touch without my permission. So, things got really bad in my household. My auntie boyfriend would always make us do crazy things. My sister used to have to wash his under clothes. This was really nasty to have a little girl wash your under wear. Like I stated before I would always find something to do at school so I would not have to go home early. Finally, school was out for the summer, I was a little mad I knew the only thing we could do was sit on the front step. We could not even walk to the store without being harassed by my aunt boyfriend when we came back. I hated to see the summer come, now tell me what child can't wait until their summer break. Well not us it was rough sometimes they made us sit in the house and we did not even have fans. I was so ready to go back to school. I prayed all summer long for school to start back this was the only freedom that I had. Summer had finally ended it was fall of 1994, school was about to begin. Yea I had passed all my classes so I was going to be a sophomore. I was excited to see all my friends from the previous year. We all decided to get our locker by each other, it was great. I and my friend Love had gym together again and we were going everyday this year. I was participating in all the activity and becoming more flexible. At this time there was nothing that I could not do in the gym. Gym became one of my favorite classes. When school let out I used to go right home do my homework and clean up the house. Some days we were not able to watch television so it would be so boring. I used to do a lot of writing and praying on my free time as you can see that all I had. I prayed every night for my mom and dad to do better so they could come and get us. It had got so bad that our punishment would be we could not go to church. My uncle used to say we were in church to long but we did not mind about being in church this was our only outlet. My sister and brother got in trouble more than I did and they would sometimes get beat. I tried my hardest to do what they said, but I felt that we were getting beat for no reason. My brother Craig played a tough role he did not care he used to get in trouble a lot. Every Sunday when we would go to church we would let people know what going on. We also told my grandmother and aunt. But everybody had a life of their own and no one had enough room for all of us. I had to make sure that all of our clothes were washed; I would have to get the old school scrubbing board. I washed all my sister and brothers' clothes on my hands. Sometimes it was hard for me going to school and trying to keep all of us up. Sometimes I would be so tried I would lose focus in school. However I thanked God every day for my siblings because what I wanted the most was for all of us to be together. Even though we stayed with grown people I still had to play the mother role. Going to school gave me the opportunity to be free. My sophomore year was so much better than the first year. I met many other people and now I knew my way around the whole school. The security guards at the school was super cool, they would let us get away with a lot of things. My best friend Robert used to beat on the locker and make all kind of music sounds. Everybody that was on our side would start dancing to the beats. It was really fun; being in school took my mind off of the things that was going on at home. Some days were good but for the most part it was frustrating. I ended up taking drivers ED and passed the written part but no one would take me for the driving part. But through it all I still stayed focused. When I became a junior in high school things became rougher. My brother Craig had just graduated out of 8th grade and he was a freshman at the same school I attended. He was skinny and small so people used to bother him just because he was little. We had to fight together a couple of times because of people messing with him. One thing about us we did not let anybody mess with us, we stood up for each other. After having those fights, it calmed down for him a little because people saw he was not afraid. Well I decide to get a job at a restaurant that was not far from where I lived. I knew I wanted something better for myself. I wanted to get my hair done and buy new shoes every now and then and also this would keep me out the house. I was tired of not having anything, so every day I left school and went to work.

It was challenging but I was very determined. They paid me under minimum wage but I did not care something beats nothing. The crazy thing was when I got paid my auntie wanted some of my money. I could not understand this for the life of me; she was already getting money for us and not buying us anything. Therefore, every time after that when I got paid I lied about how much money I had. If I did not tell a lie then I was working to give my money to someone else. My brother Craig used to also hustle, he would take out people garbage but they would hit him up also for his money. Every day we went to school we had to make it seem like we were so happy; we did not want people to know that we were miserable. My brother Craig was a character he always had people laughing he was really goofy. All the older guys at Metro High School started to like him they would say he was their little guy. My best friend Robert and brother Dennis really fell in love with him. They would make him do crazy things like go hit dude and if the guy tried to do something back they would say to the guy I wish you would. So, they always took up for him they took him under their wings. My brother looked up to them as big brothers because our oldest brother did not live with us. One day we had a talent show at our school my brother dressed up like Dennis Rodman, he sprayed painted his hair and he got on stage singing the whole school was out done. They talked about that for a minute he was the talk of the school. Everybody fell in love with him after that even the security, teachers, and his counselor. He really knew how to get to someone heart. The end of the school year was almost over with; it was time for us to go on spring break. It was crazy because the second day of spring break I caught the measles, I was so mad. It took me two weeks to get over the measles this was a miserable time for me. Finally my measles cleared up we had a month and a half before school started. I was proud of myself when I received my grades because each year I was doing better. People would always tell me I was going to be just like my mom, they said I would have a lot of kids and will not finish school. However, if people really knew me they would have had a different aspect of me. Ever since I was a little girl whatever I put my mind to I would achieve. I love to prove people wrong. The summer hit and just like every other summer we were not able to do much. My aunt was a little more lenient than the years before. The only thing that was good about the summers was that we had tons of Bar-b-cues. This was the most fun part of the summer. My uncles were chefs and loved to cook, we always looked forward to the fourth of July. My uncle and his brother used to go out of town and get fireworks and all week long they pop the fireworks until the fourth of July came around. It was amazing the whole block used to come by our house and watch it. I was scared of the fireworks I would not pop them but love to watch. One summer they were popping the fireworks my Uncle Tom was drunk he thought he threw the M80 forward but he threw it backward how come I was standing behind him and it blew up on me. I was so terrified, I was crying my leg was bleeding after that I did not want to see another firework. Then that summer me and my brother Craig and sister Alicia were walking to the Chinese restaurant, we were crossing the street and some boys was throwing fireworks and once again I got burned by fireworks. I couldn't believe that twice that summer I got burnt by fireworks. I was extremely mad that my sister and brother thought that the situation was hilarious. Nevertheless I was just ready to start school it was my last year in high school. I was going to be a senior. I had finally made it and was almost there just a little close to reaching my goal. To everyone that said I wasn't going to make it, I was ready to prove them wrong. School started back and everyone was talking about what colors they were going to wear to prom and who they were going with. I wasn't even entertaining the thought or conversation at that time because I didn't have a boyfriend and I wasn't sure if I was going to prom, so the color and who I was taking was not a concern. It was September 1996; I had the whole senior year ahead of me. A lot of things took place doing that time. In October 1996 my Uncle Larry beat my brother Craig really bad to a point where he was hurt. That same night Alisha and Craig called one of the ladies from our church where we attended name Donna. I didn't know what was going on until the next day. When I arrived to school I was called down from my third period class. I went to the office and saw my caseworker there. She was a very nice person but we never told her what was going on out of the fear of being separated again. She informed me that I had to leave with her so I left school early that day. However, when we left school she asked me what was going on because Donna had contacted her. Therefore, I start telling her everything that had been going on in that house and she ask me why we never said anything. I told her we never said anything because we did not want to be split up and that some caseworkers don't believe the kids. She stated to me that, I am taking you all out the house and did I know of any family members that would take us in. At that time, I referred Flora. She pulled Craig and Alicia out of school also and then we went to the grammar school that my younger siblings attended to pick them up. Our caseworker took us back to my auntie Joyce house to get our clothes, she told us to grab enough for the week and she would come back and get the rest. While we were there my Uncle Larry was very upset he was using all kind of profanity. He cursed us out and our caseworker, he was asking why we lie on him and my auntie Joyce. She was sitting in the living room and was not saying much about the situation. She knew everything that she was allowing to go on was wrong. My auntie was not able to look us in the face. He kept telling her Joyce say something and she replied what you want me to say. Finally, we left and went to Flora's house she decided to keep us therefore the caseworker transferred everything in her name. My caseworker was leaving and assured us she would be back in two days to take us to get the rest of our clothes. Before she left she supplied us with bus fare and lunch money to get back and forth to school. Two days later like she said she came back to get us to go and pick up our clothes. When we arrived there, we were very upset to find out that they threw all our clothes in the garbage. I was so hurt I could not believe that they would do something like that. Our caseworker asked Joyce why did they throw the clothes away and she stated because she bought them. Our auntie also stated it may be some still in the garbage can if they did not pick up the garbage yet. We had just went school shopping and she did not use her money to purchase the clothes, it was our money that the state gives us every month. Our caseworker was not a happy camper; she went back to the office and put in an emergency voucher for clothes for us. The voucher was 500 dollars and we had to split that between the six of us. Remember we did not have anything but the clothes on our back and the two outfits we had taken from the house. Now we felt like we were back to struggling again and how would we make it now. Two women from our church came over their names were Donna and Rachel. Donna and Rachel were two very special women they were known for helping people out. They came over and brought us food and also gave Flora some money. I and my sibling main focus were to finish school and this was my senior year. So, we continued to go to school and my focus was graduation. The cool thing about staying at Flora was I was able to go places; however, I was not used to this because previously I did not have freedom. My friends would come over and visit me but the funny part was I did not want to go out and party because I never did it. My best friend Robert used to throw parties in his mom's basement, they would drag me out the house just to come. So, I and a couple of friends from school start going. We also started promoting the parties at school by passing out flyers and letting them know how much it would cost. I had another friend his name was Andrew he had a crush on me and worked at McDonalds, he was really sweet. He would come to my house every night and bring me some McDonalds. We decided to go on prom together and had the colors picked out we were going to wear. But us going on prom did not quite work out that way. However, we still remained friends and even set up a trip for the senior class to go on. Well back to life, back to reality. About two months after we were staying with Flora we got evicted. One day I was walking home from school and it was a boy that was walking with me. He called himself liking me, anyhow we were about to cross the street and I look and everything in the house was sitting on the sidewalk. I turned back around and walk the other way and my cousin called me and said "Moriah" come back you know you live here. I was so embarrassed and then I had this boy that was walking with me. I got right on the phone and called Donna and Rachel and like always they were there. They helped us move some of the stuff to Flora daughter house and gave Flora some more money. These two people were really a blessing in our lives. Finally, we were settled at my auntie house and it was so crowded because she only had three bedrooms and four kids of her own. So, imagine about fourteen people staying in a three-bedroom apartment with one bathroom. We all stayed there one month before some of us started to leave and go other places. My brother Craig moved with my best friend Robert, my sister Alicia moved with one of our cousins and my other two sisters moved with Flora sister. Therefore, it was me and Julian that was still staying at the house with my grandmother and aunt. Although we did a lot of moving we still went to school and we all kept in touch with each other. The year was flying by, Christmas was approaching, like always we were not looking for anything because we never received anything on this day. Well when Christmas did arrive I decided to go out with my best friend Robert. It was about ten of us that went out and his brother Cal also came along with us. We had gone to the show and I really enjoyed myself. Robert brother Cal had been sending messages prior to all of us going out by my brother. He would tell him he liked me and how he would treat me right. I didn't know what to do beacause I was talking to someone I liked. So, while we were out on Christmas I was very impressed of how he was treating me, but kept pushing him off because I was not really interesting in talking to nobody else. After we got back from the show he asked for my number and I gave it to him. He called me that night as soon as I got in the house I think we stay on the phone for hours. So, after that we became cool and started conversating more with each other. About a month later Robert and Cal house got burnt down, my brother was staying with them. However, he had to come back home with us after this tragic incident. The good thing was nobody was hurt. Robert and his family moved with his mom daughter. I started going over there to visit them and Cal would not leave me alone. Finally, me and him started talking, at this particular time I was working at a beauty shop with another one of my best friends from church his name was Earnest, I was his shampoo girl. I used to look out for Cal because he did not have much money at the time; I would give him money for his pocket. It probably didn't mean much because I guess he was used to having money prior . But I guess he appreciated everything I had done. Anyway, he would pick me up from work every day and I would be at his house. I was at his house more than I was at home. His mom and sister were nice people and they seemed to care for me. We were really enjoying each other, eating was my favorite hobby so we stayed at the restaurants. At this point this was the person that I was taking on prom. He started back making money and he had promise me he would take care of me and that is what he did. This was my first real relationship and I was still a virgin. It took me a long time to have sex and when I did it was nothing nice it was a hurt that was unexplainable. So, I say to the young girls it's not worth it wait for your husband. I was always the type that sex did not really matter; sex was not a big issue with me. Peer pressure was very contagious back in those days. Nevertheless, time was flying by it was almost time for prom. We decided on the colors we were going to wear for prom—lime and white. I didn't want to just buy a dress, so I decided to have it made. We picked out the material, I was really excited to see it come together. As we were getting everything ready, we even found the perfect suit for Cal. Finally, prom was approaching, and I was the first person in my family to go on prom. The excitement was overwhelming. I was proud of myself because people had told me I couldn't do it—like I wasn't "worthy" of a night like this. But here I was, about to graduate out of high school and step into something bigger.

Everyone in the family came over to see me before I left. I felt a mix of nerves and excitement. I was anxious because Cal was late—something that always got to me. I wanted everything to go just right, especially on a day as important as this. This was a moment I'd been dreaming of, a chance to feel celebrated. When the doorbell rang, I almost leaped for joy—it was finally him. The nerves I had faded, and the excitement came rushing back.

As soon as Cal walked in, everyone was there, and they were already in their usual loud, boisterous fashion. My family is the kind that knows how to make everything feel like an event, and they were doing just that—shouting out into the street, "Who you with?" and all sorts of things. I was so embarrassed, but I couldn't help but laugh. I laughed so hard, tears started to run down my face. I felt like the center of attention in the best way, and for the first time in a while, I felt proud and happy. This night was already shaping up to be one of the best nights of my life.

Finally we arrived to prom, everything just clicked. My friends were there, the atmosphere was electric, we ate, danced, and just let go. For once, I felt like I was exactly where I was supposed to be. After prom, we all went to a restaurant to eat, laughing and joking around like it was the happiest moment ever. As the night winded down, we all parted ways. The next day, the tradition was to go to Great America after prom, and of course, that's exactly what we did. The whole week felt magical, along with prom, it was also my birthday week.

But then, things started to feel different. When we returned from Great America, Cal was acting strange, distant even. I couldn't put my finger on it at first, but I could sense that something was off. I tried to brush it off—after all, this was my first real relationship, and I was still figuring out the complexities of it all. But in my heart, I couldn't ignore the feeling that something wasn't right. I had this nagging sense that he was still involved with his son's mother, and that doubt kept creeping in whenever he acted differently.

One afternoon, I went to my auntie's house, and as I was leaving to go to the store, I ran into one of Cal's friends. He asked to see our prom pictures, and I didn't think much of it. I showed him the pictures, and then kept walking back home. I was feeling carefree— stomach was flat, I had on a shirt and some daisy dukes, and I was just enjoying the sunshine. But then, out of nowhere, Cal appeared. The look in his eyes was different. He came up to me, and without warning, he started pushing me. I was shocked. I had never seen this side of him before. He started accusing me of being too close to his friend, saying I was "in dude's face," but I wasn't doing anything wrong. I tried to explain myself, but he wasn't hearing me. He didn't let it go. It felt like the rug was being pulled out from under me, and I didn't understand why he was acting this way.

We got home that night, and I thought everything was fine. I was getting ready for bed when, all of a sudden, he put his foot on my neck, and I couldn't breathe. I asked him what was wrong with him, and he just replied, "Don't play with me." That should've been my red flag right then and there. I should've realized this man was crazy.

However, the next morning, he left before I did, so I took that chance to pack up all my things and called a cab. But before I knew it, he came back to the house and asked me what I was doing. I quickly lied and told him I was taking my clothes over to my auntie's house to wash them. He believed me and offered to drop me off.

When I got to my auntie's house, I told her everything that had happened. Everyone was furious, and they all wanted to know why I hadn't left sooner. I told my aunt that if he called, she should just say I was sleeping. So, my sister Alicia and I decided to walk to the store. Outside, people were having a water gun fight, and as soon as we walked up to the door, Cal and his friends soaked us with water. We were so mad.

We walked to the store, bought water guns of our own, and went back home. We filled up the guns and even grabbed some big buckets to make sure we could really get them good. I called Cal to the door, making him think we were going to talk about what happened. He walked up like a fool, and we drenched him with water. He couldn't say anything except, "You got me good."

Later that night, he called and somehow convinced me to come back to his house. He apologized, saying he would never hit me again, that he didn't know what had gotten into him, and that he was sorry. I was young, naïve, and didn't know any better, so I went back. Even though I knew deep down it wasn't right, I believed him because I wanted to.

Ladies, let me tell you something—if a man hits you once, he will do it again. It's never just a one-time thing.

But if you keep reading, you'll see it never stopped. Everything was going well—his family bought a new house, and we moved in with his mom. I stayed there just until DCFS gave me my own apartment. We stayed at his mom's house from June 1997 until November of 1997, and during that time, I was approved for independent living. I found a studio apartment that I absolutely fell in love with. There's truly nothing like having your own space. So, in November 1997, we moved out completely, and things were still going well. He would come home every night, and we'd always go somewhere together.

But then, the relationship started to take a turn. He said he was working a night job, but I started to notice it wasn't true. He began staying out later, and we weren't spending much time together anymore. Sometimes, when he'd come home, his phone would ring constantly, but he'd never answer it. There was this one number that kept showing up on his phone, and we were sharing the same line. When my bill came in the mail, I noticed that number appeared more times than my own.

I think as young women, we can be so naïve. We know something's going on, but we don't want to face it because of that thing called love. I'd been hearing rumors that he was cheating, but sometimes, you need to see things for yourself before you can accept the truth. One night, he didn't come home, so I decided to call that number. My first instinct was to get my brother, Craig, to call and ask to speak to Cal. When a woman answered, she handed the phone right to him—clearly, he was right there with her. I think she must've assumed it was one of his brothers or friends calling because, who else would be calling her phone?

When he said hello, both my brother and I just hung up.

Thirty minutes later he came in the house screaming and acting crazy saying I mess things up for him. I don't know how he knew that was me calling. I knew he was lying but he started to fight me, he pulled out my hair and put my head in the toilet stool. He was trying to drown me, after that he choked me unconscious but kept slapping me and putting water and my face to wake me up. After he did this he took the phone bill and burned it up and forced me to have sex with him. I could not believe that I was going through this; every day I thought to myself what did I do to deserve this. My thought process was I have been abused from childhood up until now Lord what have I done so wrong. But in spite of everything I went through I ask God to give me strength. I prayed so hard to God to bring me out of the situation, I knew I deserved better. I called my church and my friend Sally and some other people came to pick me up from home. I was so ashamed of what happen to me but all the time I was crying out for help. We have to know that when someone is crying out because if we don't pay attention then some people may lose their life. The only thing I would hear is people saying I can't go through that or I would have left the man a long time ago. Like I told some people once and I will tell anybody don't say what you will or will not do because you are not in that situation but if a person is I wanted to see how easy it is to get up and walk. Especially when a person knows your every move. I knew this man was destroying my life, I stayed on my knees or in my bed praying to God to show me the way out. He was crazy, he knew where I was at all times and I was not afraid at first but as time went on I was very scared. After that incident I stayed at my auntie's house for a couple of days but I went back because I was scared and did not want my family to be involved. I always would tell them what happen because if something happen to me they would know who did it. I had called the police on several occasions but he told me if I call them again he would kill me. I was really trusting God to work this situation out because if you really want to know the truth it was out of the hands of man. Like I said before if a man hit you once it does not stop. So, I went to my house, things were still the same he would buy me things I guess he thought that made me happy. Materials things should not make anyone happy they come and go. So I got a phone call from my friends Sally and Malcolm they wanted to go out and eat. These were my two best friends and we always ate together. After leaving the restaurant a particular song came on I was really feeling it. The name of the song was,

I'm not your Superwoman". I told Sally and Malcolm I was tired and I was packing my stuff and leaving. They ask me are you serious. I was crying I did not know how I was going to do it but I was going to try. One day I was sitting at home and I said to myself what can I say or do to leave. I started working and I was not trying to depend on no one anymore, then something clicked in my brain. I already had my own apartment and did not have to pay a dime for my rent so I decided I would tell him I would move because I did not sign my lease. I know someone might say they won't make you move for that they would just ask you to sign. Well he did not know no better and certainly did not know how to take care of business. Therefore, I called my aunt to see if I could stay with her and pay her 50 dollars a week. She said yes so, I called Cal and told him I had to move, he said okay and bought the lie. We both moved all our stuff out the house it really didn't make a difference to me because he was not coming home anyway. He took me to my auntie house and left. Things were going well; I called Cal and told him to bring my television over to my auntie house. When he called my brother answered and told him I was not there. So, I called him back and he started talking crazy, he was saying what kind of games are you playing? Is that why you moved to your auntie house because you want to cheat? So, I hung up the phone, a couple hours later he came over to bring the television. I went outside to open the door and he said he was taking me to his mom house. Instantly a feeling came across me. I felt like he was going to fight me. I told him I did not want to go, and then he asked me what you mean, I couldn't explain. I attempted to open the door and he grabbed me and started beating me. He pulled me down concrete stairs and stomp my head with some Timberland boots. He beat me unconscious, I woke up once and I was in my auntie house and then passed back out. The second time I gained conscious I was in the ambulance but passed out again. They had to use the defibrillators to bring me back. When we got to the hospital I was conscious but did not remember anything that had happen. Kathy came to the hospital and she was crying when she saw me and I told her mom please don't cry I'm okay. Finally, I was able to go the bathroom and I saw myself I started to cry I looked so bad. He had pulled my hair and I had a ball spot in the middle of my head, my face was so big. I could not believe he beat me like that. All I could think of again is what have I done so wrong. Nobody in my auntie house did nothing to him they let him do this to me, maybe because they were afraid of him also, but I almost lost my life. We finally made it back to my auntie house when we got there I sat in the tub for hours because I was hurting so bad. He was so bold he kept calling the house all that night and wanting to speak to me. I did not know that a person who says they love you but can hurt you so bad. At this point in my life I felt like what's next, I been hurt all my life. Was I ever going to be happy? I just wanted to be happy ever since I was a little girl. I truly found out that you cannot find happiness in a man it's in God. This occurred around

Thanksgiving time this is when we supposed to be grateful for what God has done for us and thankful for each other. Well I guess this was the other way around my thanks was given to me differently. Months went by and I still did not talk to him and he kept calling my auntie house every day. I started going out on dates with this guy I went to junior college with his name was Keith he was a good friend. Every time I went out I felt like I had to watch my surrounding to make sure I don't run into him. Keith was cool to be around did not like him much. However, I had to do something to keep my mind off Cal. Well I was still staying at my auntie and my cousin Tammy had come over to stay also. She had two kids and had just broken up with her boyfriend. She was not comfortable over there so I offered to get an apartment together. I was still in independent living and they would pay my rent until I turned 21 years of age. We started looking for an apartment and finally we found one it was right around the corner from my auntie who I was currently staying with. We came to an agreement that I would let DCFS pay the rent and she would pay me her half. We moved in and things were going great I was still working therefore I was straight. But I had messed up again I ran into Cal and we would talk every now and then, for Valentine Day he came to my job and brought me some flowers and a diamond ring. I was stunned and it seemed too good to be true. However, the same day he also delivered flower and a ring to the person he was cheating with me on before. I was hurt a little because I was not over him all the way. Sometimes in life God gives us signs but we choose not to recognize them. We second guess ourselves knowing that what we seen or heard is right most of the time. They always say the first person you are with is the hardest to get over. But I always knew after a while that we were not going to be together forever, this was no longer the man for me. I began to talk to this guy from my church I used to talk to him all the time, we became the best of friends. He was my big brother; I was able to go to him with anything. That same night when Cal took the other girl out for Valentine Day, my friend Malcolm bought me a teddy bear. When he got to the house I showed him the ring. He was like that's nice but I know he did not care for Cal much because he knew about all the things that he was and had done to me. Everybody in my family disliked him but it is not unusual in a family. If your family loves you then they do not want to see you hurt. Anyhow me and Cal would still talk on the phone or I would go see him every once in a while. I wouldn't let anyone know because I knew I shouldn't be seeing him. Even though it was like once a month. One day me and my cousin decided to throw a party at our new apartment, we just wanted everyone to come over and kick it. Me and my cousin invited our friends and family over. I invited friends from the church and outside the church. On the day of the party I was doing a lot of running around. This particular day; I had to get all the stuff for the party. I invited Cal, (why did I do this) his brother and one of his sisters who I was really cool with. After running around, I went back home just to find out from my cousin that the lights went out. I went downstairs to flip the fuse box back on and in the process, I was shocked. Everything that I had in my other had fell to the floor. The shock caused a vibrating sensation in my fingers which scared me. I ran back upstairs to tell my cousin what I was feeling because this was an unusual feeling and situation for me. Once the feeling was back to normal I begin to clean the house. I started cleaning my room and on that particular day my prom glass had fallen and broke. I thought that was unusual because it had fallen before but never broke. This was very strange because there was carpet in my room. Nevertheless, I cleaned it up and continued to clean the rest of the room. I finished cleaning just in time for the party to begin.

Everyone begin to arrive the music was playing and we all begin to dance. The dance that was popular that particular year was the Cha-Cha slide so that's what we were doing, the Cha-cha Slide. Finally, Cal came in and he was upset and we weren't together anymore so I didn't understand why. He asked me if we could talk so I went in my room with him and as usual he begins to talk crazy so I left out and went back where everyone was partying. He eventually came out and my friend Starlette asked him why was he so upset?

He never answered and just walked out the door. A few minutes later he came back and pulled me in the washroom. Again, Cal begins to act and talk crazy with the name calling. The knocks on the door begin because people needed to use the washroom. I was so glad, I left out and begin to dance again but Cal left out the house. I went to my room and everyone came in there to check to see if I was okay and I was. About five minutes later he returned and ran right into my bedroom and places his hand up on my stomach. I was terrified. I forgot that he carries a gun so all my friends and cousins begin to jump on him. Once again, he left and this time when he returned he had the gun with him.

Everyone ran out the back door and I took them to the room with the fuse box. I knew he wouldn't find us there because it was really dark there, we were all safe. I begin to thank God because if the fuse wouldn't have gone out earlier that day I wouldn't have known where to run for safety. That day was the very first time I've been downstairs in that area, God knew. Cal sister came over later that day and I told her everything that happened and to my amaze he told her that the party was cancelled because he didn't want her to stop him from acting crazy with me. I called the police and they arrived shortly after his sister arrived. I made a police report and everyone went home. The party was over. The very next day made me realize that I was no longer safe so I decided that I would go to Memphis with my aunt for a few weeks to get away. My friend Malcolm came over and spent the whole day with me. We watched movies and just relaxed. Days went by and I decided that I needed to move out from the place I was living. I told my cousin and she was upset that I made that decision however I didn't feel safe there anymore. I couldn't understand why she was so upset because she didn't have to pay anything she had a free ride. She broke in my room and took all of my perfume and body wash it was well over five hundred dollars in value. I was so upset I left out and went where my brother was and told him what happened. He went back to the house with me to get the rest of my things. My cousin begins to talk crazy which cause a huge fight between us. I and my brother were fighting my cousin and her sister. That was the day I was leaving to go to Memphis to stay with my aunt for a few weeks. I was so sad and confused. Everything was packed and ready. My friend Lovely came and stayed with me the whole day until Malcolm arrived to take me to the bus station.

Finally made it to Memphis, my aunt picked me up from the bus station and we headed to her house. I was amazed at how different things were from Chicago. I never had been there before. I was excited and sad at the same time. I was excited to see all my cousins but sad that I left my family and church family back in Chicago. A few days went by and I begin to get bored I was ready to come back home. Cal was calling my phone telling me how sorry he was but his sorry didn't mean anything at this point. I knew I didn't deserve the treatment that I was receiving. When you learn to love yourself first then you will not allow anyone else to treat you any different. I was looking for love my parents weren't around, living from house to house, shelter to shelter to foster homes. Every placed we stayed we were treated badly. In my search for love I met Cal and he promised me everything that I was looking for but treated me bad like everyone else did, I realized later that isn't what love is. My aunt Laura was nice; she was the only aunt on my father side that would come visit us. No matter what I knew my aunt loved me and anything I ever needed I could depend on her. Aunt Laura was the strong woman of the family on my father side; she was raising her sister's kids at the time. While in Memphis she took me several places and she also took me to the beauty salon to get my hair fixed. Those two weeks seem like two years at the time because I was ready to go home. Well the day came and it was time for my aunt to take me to the bus station to head home to Chicago and when I arrived Malcolm was there to pick me up. On the way home Malcolm and I had a very long conversation. I told him after all I went through, all I could think of is I never wanted to be in another relationship with a man. However, Malcolm always would listen and show signs that he cared about me and my siblings.

CHAPTER 3
ADULTHOOD

I finally arrived to my aunt house where everyone was so excited to see me back home. She told me that I could stay with her until I got back on my feet. I searched in the newspapers for jobs every day and it seems like if you lacked experience you weren't going to get the job, but I kept searching. Malcolm would come by my aunt house almost every day to hang out and teach me how to drive but, I was nervous to learn. Cal never tried teaching me how to drive because he didn't want me to get around. It was a shame the amount of money I've spent paying for cab rides. I could have bought a new car. Seeing that Malcolm was trying to teach me made me promise myself that I would learn. After a long search of looking for jobs, I finally found a job through an agency. It was in the downtown Chicago area working for the IRS making fifteen dollars an hour. I asked Malcolm to take me downtown because I didn't know my way around. The job was easy but it only lasted a week. The supervisors came in and told us that all the work was complete and we could go home. It was three o'clock in the morning and I didn't have a way home. I had to wait until five o'clock that morning because the trains in downtown Chicago stop running after one a.m. I didn't have a cell phone and the stores were all closed and I didn't have any more coins for the phone. This whole situation had depressed me because I had to stay with my aunt for three more months. I found another job doing telemarketing and it paid eight dollars an hour. I couldn't afford to give her much because it was part-time. Things begin to get bad at my aunt house she was listening to other when it came to the things about me and she put me out. I couldn't afford my own place at the time making the money I was making wasn't enough. I ended up in Indiana staying with the woman I was working for. I was bored living there and it was very difficult for me to get around, I didn't know how to drive. I came back to Chicago and ended up living with my brother David girlfriend who was living with her sister. I had to get her permission to stay there and she was okay with me being there. The job wasn't working out how I thought it would. I wasn't seeing any cash flow. That made me look for another job which was frustrating situation, but God always made a way. The girl that lived downstairs told me about a CNA class and she referred me and my brothers' girlfriend. We both went to fill out the application and we both got called back to start the class which lasted for six weeks. This class had certain stipulations that we had to agree with. I payed the fee and patiently waited for the class to start. We had to sign an agreement that we would work there for at least one year because it was a free class. I passed the test and worked there for two years. While I was working there I got my own apartment and things begin going well for me. I moved back into the building where my first apartment was. I was there for about three months and my sister Dee came to live with me. She stayed with me for a while. Afterwards my Aunt Laura came to visit with my cousins and one of my cousins ended up staying with me for about a year. That was in 2001 the same year Alicia came home from college. She was home sick. She never went back because the school messed up her paperwork. So now in my apartment it was me, my little cousin and Alicia staying in a studio apartment. We were there for a few months and I decided to get a one-bedroom apartment. Alicia and I applied to go to the same college where she studied business and I studied criminal justice. Everything was going great between Alicia and I. Although I struggled taking care of us I never gave up and still worked at the nursing home. Alicia didn't have a job at the time. Also I had the responsibility of enrolling my little cousin in school and getting all the things she needed to start school.

In March of that year I got a job with my cousin working at Maryhill paying $10.82 an hour. I thought I was really doing big things then. I knew this job would allow me to have extra money. Everything started to go uphill in my life then four months later, something drastic happened. But, three months before it happened I kept telling my aunt that I was dreaming about death in the family and I kept telling her that someone was going to die. I didn't know who. On April 16, 2002 my sister Alicia got a phone call on her cell phone. She was in the living room and I was in the bedroom. I heard her say he got shot. At that moment my stomach started to turn. I kept calling her name asking her who got shot. She said our brother Craig; I was trying to stay calm. I asked where was he and she said that they were taking him to Cook County Hospital. We all jumped in the car, Cathy said she would drive because she knew I was too nervous too but, she was nervous as well. I thought I was going to die on the way there from the way she was driving. We when arrived to the hospital they informed us that the ambulances hadn't even arrived with him. I was asking some of the other family members what happened and they said he got shot in the back. I prayed Lord please don't let my brother be paralyzed. Twenty minutes later the ambulance arrived but the sirens were off. I then prayed Lord please don't let him be dead. When they took him out of the ambulance Kathy immediately asks if that was Craig. They asked if he had a tattoo on his arm and my mom said yes. They took her in the back room and we didn't hear anything from anyone for about thirty minutes. Everyone was at the hospital our pastor, family and friends. I was walking around the hospital nervous as ever then I heard my cousin Tammy scream. They had pronounced Craig dead. I couldn't believe my brother was gone, I said God this can't be true. I begin to cry and I broke down this news caused both Alicia and Flora to faint. Craig got killed on a Tuesday, everyone just saw him that Easter Sunday at the church and over by my aunt house. That Sunday Craig had brought his girlfriend by the house so everyone could meet her. That Monday he called me playing on the phone and I didn't know it was him playing until he said sister. All this was going thru my head it was unbelievable that he was dead. The family stayed at the hospital until three a.m. we were all heartbroken. When we left the hospital we all went to my Aunt Toya house, nobody could sleep so we decided to go to the area where he got shot and put up a memorial and then I went home. I called my aunt Laura from Memphis to give her the news and she left to come to Chicago immediately to be with the family. Everyone including the pastor and our first lady was coming by my place the next day I tried to be strong but it was really hard. Craig didn't have any life insurance so we had to get money from every resource we could to bury Craig. Thank God that our Pastor had friends that owned a funeral home which really helped us out. During this time I still couldn't believe Craig was not with us any longer. This was the brother that I went through childhood life struggles with. When things got hard for us we always stuck together we all just wanted to be happy. I wanted the week to go by fast so we could have the funeral and let the healing process begin. The day of the funeral everyone was at my house, there was a sad feeling in the atmosphere in the entire house. We were all nervous nobody ate or said anything. The funeral started at ten we all were dressed sitting around and some were taking pictures waiting for the limo to pick us up. When the limo came I and Alicia begin to cry before we even got to the church. Finally we arrived to the church we took our time getting out but the family was waiting on us to procession in. We walked in the church and everyone was in tears but I was trying to stay strong, however when I got to the casket I couldn't believe my brother Craig was laying there. I touched his face and kissed him, he did not look the same he was big and swollen.

They closed the casket and the service had begun, the choir sung and we joined in. Most of our family was in the choir so God gave us the strength to sing along with them. During the funeral a couple of people in our family carried out terrible it was funny and embarrassing at the same time. My sister Leanna had an asthma attack, Alicia got scared and fainted, my cousin Adriane ran to the front screaming granny Alicia is about to die. I was so embarrassed after the funeral my cousin Adriane ran out of the church up and down the streets yelling my cousin Craig is dead over and over again. It was a sad and embarrassing moment that day. Afterwards we all went over my aunt Toya house for the repast where everyone came by to visit. I was so glad that this day was over with. I went home and finally got comfortable then the doorbell ranged. I went downstairs and there was Cal standing there. He asked if we could talk and I agreed. He begins to talk crazy as usual which really upset me because we just buried my brother. I was at a point in my life where I stood him in the face and told him where he could get off at the next stop. I didn't care anymore and I wasn't scared any longer. My fears toward Cal were over. I had just experienced the scariest thing in life losing my brother. At that point I and Cal weren't together anyway so I went back upstairs with my family and relaxed. My aunt Laura was still here, she stayed until Friday. But after she left I was scared and lonely but thank God my sister Leanna and my cousin Sherry was living with me. When Laura left I tried to go back to sleep but I kept hearing noises like someone was in the house. I jumped up out of bed and went into the living room but everyone was still asleep. I woke up Leanna and told her to come lay in the bed with me. At that time the noise came back and we both heard it. I believed it was my brother spirit walking through the house but it didn't matter because I was scared. I got some clothes and headed to my aunt house for the weekend. It seemed like everything begin to go wrong after he died. My car died out, I got behind on rent because I had to pay for some things for his funeral which were very pricey. Alicia and my cell phones got turned off because our bill got so high from calling everyone when Craig died. I begin to get frustrated. I begin to pray to God for a lot of things but I really asked him to help me take care of my brothers and sisters. We all at that time were staying in my one-bedroom apartment. I was trying to get Leanna back into school and at the same time was struggling with my little brother. I also prayed for God to take Cal out of my life. I begin to look for a bigger place and I didn't need the extra stress that Cal had to offer. One day my friend Rachel who was more like a big sister called me and said that there was an empty apartment next door to where she lived. Her step father knew the guy who was renting the apartment so he said that I could rent the apartment. I think he was a little scared because I was young and I told him that I took care of my sisters and brothers and they were going to be staying with me. The rent was a thousand dollars a month so I had to come up with twenty-five hundred dollars before I could move in. I didn't know where I was going to get the money from. A guy by the name of Kenneth gave me the rest of the money that I needed to move in. I thank God for him and his wife they had the heart to help everyone. Kenneth also taught me how to drive and took me to get my driver's license. Anyway, I moved in the apartment in May of 2003. I left my other apartment to my sister Dee and William. What I do that for they did not pay the rent and I ended up getting an eviction on my credit report? I was so mad and embarrassed. Sometimes you cannot help family because they would leave you out there bogus all the time. When I moved to Maywood things were going well. My ex-boyfriend did not know where I was, me and my siblings were happy. It was hard but we were striving to make things work out for us. Two weeks after I moved in I sent my little cousin Sherry back to Memphis with my auntie she did not want to act right. I kept her for a year and a half. School was about to begin so I had to register my sister Pearl in Providence East, that was the high school that was across the street from us. She did not give me any problems everything

I asked her she did. My sister Alicia was working at Wendy's and going to school. We were both going to Manely X College but when we moved, we registered at Titan College. I was working ten hours shift a day and I was also a full-time student. The only thing I would think about is that I was going to make it. I wanted a degree and no matter what I was going to get it. Even though I was tired I kept pressing. A couple of months after I moved in my brother Julian got out of jail he came home on house arrest. I had to take several days off work to get my brother settled into school, and it was getting really frustrating. My job was patient with me, but it was a lot to manage. On top of that, I had to run back and forth to court for him every month. Even when he got out, things didn't improve. He was still acting out, sneaking in and out of my window at all hours of the night, and one day, he even cut off his house arrest bracelet. It was insane—when I came home from work one day, the box and bracelet were just sitting in front of my door. The first thing that crossed my mind was that something wasn't right with him. But despite everything, I tried to be there for my siblings. I had made a promise to them, and I was determined to keep it.

When I moved to Maywood, everyone came to stay with me—my siblings, friends from church, and others we knew. We had so much fun in Maywood. We played games, goofed off, and hung out like it was the best spot in the world. I only stayed there for about a year, but six months in, I let William come live with me. He had just gotten out of jail, and I needed help paying the rent. When he got out, he came into some money, but instead of keeping it all to himself, he gave some to each of my siblings. He gave me the most since I was the oldest. We went shopping and had a good time with the money, and I even gave a little to my friends.

But as time went on, I started feeling defeated when it came to my siblings. I was the only one working, and my sister Alicia quit her job and stopped going to school for a semester. Every day, I'd come home, the house would be full of people. I wasn't mad about that, but I was upset because the house was never clean. I can't stand a messy house, and after working all day, I expected a little help. But every day, it was the same routine. One day, I got so fed up that I took all the dishes out of the cabinets—pots, pans, silverware—and put them in my room. I told everyone, "If nobody wants to wash the dishes, then nobody should use them." I was still trying to be reasonable, though, and left one plate, bowl, spoon, and fork for each person, telling them to take turns eating out of it to see how it felt.

Taking care of someone else's kids is tough, especially when you don't have any of your own, and even tougher when they don't appreciate what you're doing. My sister Alicia started getting more disrespectful, and I reached my breaking point. One day, after the same routine of frustration, I told her to pack her things and leave. That was painful for me because I didn't want to do it, but I had to show tough love. About a month later, she found out she was pregnant, and I felt a little guilty for putting her out. But after that, I ended up putting everyone out. Things weren't improving, and it was getting too difficult.

My brother Julian was giving me a hard time, and my little brother Kenon was hard to manage. Raising boys was harder than I thought. Eventually, I put my dad out, too, and told Julian he couldn't come back. So, it ended up just being me, my sister Leanna, and my brother Kenon living in my apartment. Things were getting harder for me, especially financially. I wasn't making as much money anymore, and I was struggling to pay the rent. At that point, I was making only $10.82 an hour, but I was still trying to buy a house for my siblings, hoping to give them a place to live. Even though I could barely cover my own bills, by God's grace, I managed to keep up with the rent and my car payment.

Then, the summer of 2003, school was out, and my little brother Kenon moved back in with the woman he'd stayed with before. But things with my sister Leanna were starting to unravel. She wasn't listening to me, was acting out, and wanted to do her own thing. By this point, I felt like I had given everything I could, but it still wasn't enough. I felt unappreciated, and it was hard to keep going when nothing was getting better.

I found myself in a really tough spot when I had to move out of my apartment because I simply couldn't afford it anymore. So, I began looking for another place, but then a friend of mine reached out with an idea that seemed like a lifeline. Her mom was moving out of her house, and she asked me if I wanted to share the space with her, splitting the rent in half. At first, it felt like a great solution—an opportunity to save money but it quickly turned into one of the biggest mistakes I ever made.

I moved out of my old apartment and moved in with my friend, along with my sister. We signed the lease, got everything notarized, and thought things were going to work out. But that's where things started to fall apart. My friend and I had an agreement that no men would stay overnight and there wouldn't be different men coming in and out the house. However, this was quickly violated. Conflicts began to arise between me, my friend, and her sister, mostly due to their boyfriends constantly being around—and worst of all, they weren't contributing anything to the rent.

On top of that, my sister had started talking to my friend's brother, and everything just seemed to spiral. My sister, who I thought I could trust, began talking badly about me behind my back, and the betrayal hurt deeply. I felt like I was losing everyone around me. To make matters worse, about a month after moving in, my best friend—who had been staying there—moved out without warning. One day, while I was home asleep, I received a text from her saying she was leaving because she couldn't take living there anymore. She was moving in with her baby's father. I was blindsided and devastated. I called her immediately, but her decision was final. I couldn't believe it.

The situation continued to get worse when my friend's mom called me and told me I could still stay there for $500 a month. That felt like a huge relief at the time, and I was thankful. But then, just two weeks later, she called me again to say her brother was taking over the house, and I had to move out. This time, there was no negotiation. I had to be out in a week. I was crushed. Finding a new place to live, especially in Chicago, was nearly impossible. I cried for hours, asking myself, "What else could possibly go wrong?"

Desperately I started making calls. I reached out to a friend from church who lived in Joliet, and she told me there were apartments available in her building. I didn't want to move that far out, but it was the only option I had at that moment. I filled out an application and hoped for the best. Two days later, I got a call saying I had been approved. I went back to the complex, paid the deposit, and was able to move into my new apartment. The timing couldn't have been more perfect, and to top it off, I got a month's rent free as part of a move-in special.

That weekend, I packed up everything and moved. It felt like a fresh start, though it was bittersweet because I had to leave my sister behind. She thought she could manage on her own, but within a month, they kicked her out too. It was hard to watch her go through the same thing, but sometimes, you have to let people see things for themselves. I wasn't going to keep her with me because I had to look out for myself, even though I was hurt by her actions and words.

Despite all the chaos with family and friends, I had one person who stood by me—my best friend. People assumed we were in a relationship, but he was just my closest friend. In 2003, things started to change between us. I never saw him in that way, but he didn't give up. Slowly, we started dating, and although he wasn't the kind of guy I thought I wanted, he was my rock. We had built such a deep connection over the years that eventually, we couldn't deny what was there.

I tried to stay positive, even when things felt so heavy. After everything went down with my sister, I let her move in with me, even though I had every right to be angry. I didn't want to hold grudges, and I did my best to help her. She was going to be a senior in high school, so I registered her at the school nearby. I wasn't perfect, but I tried to do right by her.

When I first moved to Joliet, I had quit my job because the commute was unbearable. I was out of work for a couple of months, but I didn't let it stop me. I found a new job by October, but the schedule was grueling. I had to work the night shift to accommodate my school schedule, and I was going to school four nights a week. The exhaustion was unreal. There were times I would go into work, but my body was so worn out that I'd have to leave after just a few hours. It was like my body just couldn't keep up. But even through all that, I kept going. By some miracle, everything worked out. Bills got paid on time, my car note was always covered, and I had food on the table. It was clear to me that God had been with me through all the hardships. Without His guidance, I honestly don't know how I would've made it through.

In October 2003, I still was able to go on my cruise, despite everything I had going on. But let me just say this: God is so good. When I reflect on everything He brought me through—the trials and tribulations—I can only count them as blessings. Life was challenging, but looking back, it was clear that every step had a purpose.

During that time, I was working every night and also getting my sister, Leanna, ready for her graduation and prom. She graduated in May of 2004, and I was set to graduate in December of that same year. It was a year of hard work for both of us. After she graduated, I realized that commuting from Joliet to Chicago every other day had become too much. The suburbs were nice, but it wasn't where I felt at home. I loved the energy of Chicago, even though people often say it's dangerous and chaotic. Sure, I felt that way sometimes, but I came to believe that whether you're in the suburbs or the city, it's about your mindset. It's what you make it, and I knew I needed to be where I felt alive.

So, I moved back to Chicago, with only one semester left to graduate. I enrolled at a city college, Manley X College, and took two classes there, while still completing another class at Joliet Junior College. My sister, Leanna, wanted to be more independent, so I told her she couldn't stay with me. But before I moved, my little cousin from Memphis came up for the summer, and she stayed with me during that time.

A friend rented me an apartment at an affordable price, and soon, my godbrother decided to move in with me. We became roommates. The rent was incredibly cheap—probably the lowest I had ever paid for an apartment—and I was happy about it. Things were going pretty well with the new setup. The only downside was that my godbrother wasn't as clean as I was, so we'd occasionally clash about it. But he was family, and we worked through it.

I had quit my job when I left Joliet, and by June 2004, I found myself unemployed again. I know what you're probably thinking: "She's always quitting her job!" But you know what? That's okay because in July, God blessed me with a job at the telephone company NBC (ST&T). However, the job came with its own challenges. I had already planned a trip before I got hired, but the company said I couldn't go. That felt unfair, especially because I had already paid for it. It was a tough moment, but I decided to go on the trip anyway. When I came back, I was ready to quit, but after reflecting on it, I chose to stay and make the most of the opportunity.

I worked there from July 2004 until March 2005. Balancing that job with school was hard, especially since the job had strict attendance rules. With my graduation on the horizon, I was juggling my time between Chicago and Joliet, barely keeping my head above water. But the hard work paid off. The day of my graduation was one of the happiest days of my life. I had worked so hard to achieve this goal, and no matter the obstacles I faced, I was determined to cross the finish line.

I want to take a moment to speak directly to anyone reading this—especially young men and women who may feel like the world is against them. It doesn't matter if your parents were absent or if you were a ward of the state. What matters is that you put your mind to something and trust that God will guide you. You can achieve anything you want, regardless of the circumstances. Believe in yourself, even if you're not an "A" student or the perfect candidate for success. Hard work always pays off.

My story isn't just about the struggles, though—it's about the faith I held onto and the belief that I could rise above any challenge. There were moments when I doubted myself, but I kept pushing forward, knowing that every step was leading me to something greater. When I walked acrossed that stage at graduation, I felt a sense of pride like never before. It wasn't just about the diploma—it was about everything I had overcome to get to that point. And I knew, in that moment, that nothing was impossible as long as I kept my faith and kept working hard.

When I graduated I did not graduate with honors, I went to school knowing that I had did my best and I got "C 's" but I worked hard for that "C" and got my degree. I was proud of my grades because I knew I worked hard to get them so I praised God for every one of them. Like I stated before I had to work and attend school but guess what I never failed one class. Therfore you can accomplish anything you want just put your mind and heart into it look at me. Graduation was special to me and people that love me came, also my boyfriend Malcolm was there, we had grown closer in our friendship and relationship. I knew this was the man for me but at the time I was so afraid to talk to him because at first, I did not like him I just always looked at him as a brother, but he never stopped coming around and kept trying. He would tell me I'm going to get you, and my response was it is not going to be easy.

And guess what it was not easy for him he will tell you that. But we finally got together in the year of 2003. However everyone made graduation day special for me most of all I had to thank God for giving me the strength to make it. During that time, I was still working for NBC which is now ST&T. I was looking for jobs in my field but as you know when you graduate it is strange how you cannot find a job. I got fired from my job in March of 2005 it wasn't anything I could do about it. I had to go to court and I was not able to miss any more days at work. So, after I lost my job I went to the unemployment office. It was not so bad keeping up with the bills because I had a roommate. We split all the bills in the house. My unemployment check wasn't much but it paid my bills I was getting a little anxiety with sitting home, because I wasn't use to that and I felt like I needed more money, so I started babysitting for one of my cousins, it wasn't much money but she needed the help, I was off work until October 2005. A lot of crazy things were happening. My boyfriend was in a motorcycle accident which scared the mess out of me. He could have died but God saw fit for him to be here. When I got that call, I rushed to the hospital the first thing that was going through my mind was God don't take him away from me. The accident was crucial he went in the air and came down on the bike and this happened on the expressway. When he walked out of the hospital he didn't not have one scratch on him. I really thank God for that because he did not have to do it. But if you know my boyfriend he is a rider, he did not stay off that bike. All I could do was pray and ask God to cover him. Then a couple of months later something else happened, it was in August I was at my god brother's birthday party and I kept calling my boyfriend which is now my husband. But the phone kept saying the Nextel subscriber you are trying to reach cannot be located. So, I said what is going on he was supposed to stop by but I did not think anything else of it. About forty minutes later his friend Joey chirped me I did not recognize the chirp number so I said who is this he replied Moriah this is Joey, Malcolm just got shot in the back. Instantly my heart drop I was nervous I ran up the stairs to put my shoes on my friend Kayla drove me to the hospital

She was the same person who took me to the hospital when he had the motor cycle accident. When I arrived at the hospital all his friends and family was there. I ran into his mother and she said he just ask about you go back there so you can see him. When I went back there he was calm but you can tell that he was in pain. The nurse was telling him that they had to cut open his stomach to get the bullet out. His whole facial expression changed. The bullet had traveled and stopped right at his main artery if the bullet would have moved anymore he could have died. I was scared the first thing that came to mind was my brother and how he got shot and died. I begin to pray to God again, asking Him not to take him away. I kissed him, and then they took him into surgery. My friends came up to the hospital, and we all waited together for a long time. But I stayed by his side from eleven that night until two-thirty the next day. I sat in his room with him until the end. He had many visitors, I was so tired. I knew I needed to go home to rest, but I wasn't ready to leave him. He stayed in the hospital for four days. During that time, every day I made sure he was clean, and I made sure the nurses did their jobs as well. The nurses started to get annoyed with me, and they even tried to get me to leave the hospital, but I wouldn't. I needed to be there for him.

Fortunately, he did well in therapy, and they eventually released him. Both of us were relieved, and for a moment, we felt a sense of peace. I called my sister Alicia, and she came to pick us up from the hospital. He went home to his mother's house because he was still weak and needed assistance. So, I stayed with him, making sure he was well taken care of. This was one of the hardest times of my life, but I stayed strong through it all.

During this difficult period, my godbrother—whom I had been sharing an apartment with—suddenly decided to move out and get married without even informing me. I was stunned. At the same time, I had lost my job and couldn't find another one. Malcolm was unable to work either. Everything seemed to be falling apart, and I couldn't help but wonder, "What else could go wrong?" My unemployment benefits were running out, and I was growing increasingly frustrated as I struggled to find a job.

I spoke to my landlord and explained that I might need to move out if I couldn't get back on my feet financially. I didn't want to burden her, especially when she has her own bills to pay. I promised her I would move if I couldn't find a job soon. So, I kept searching, and I ended up putting my resume back in at my old job.

Then, two days later, I got the call: they offered me the job. It felt like a miracle. I'd been doubting for so long, but I learned that God's timing is perfect. Even when we doubt, He is always working behind the scenes. I'm a testament to the truth that God provides for us, even when we don't see how. He will never give us more than we can bear. His promises are real, and He always delivers—if only we believe.

So, when you are going through different situations remember what God said and from that thought you know that you are going to come out of it. I am more than a conqueror through Christ Jesus, who strengthens me.

I began my job in October 2005. At first, I wasn't interested in it at all. Honestly, I didn't care much for it. But God has a way of humbling you, of breaking you down, and then bringing you right back into the same situation— so you can learn the lessons you missed the first time. That's exactly what happened to me. We often take the small things for granted, not realizing how important they really are. But God cannot bless us with the big things if we're not grateful for the little ones. I had to change my perspective, realign my heart, and rediscover what truly mattered. Once I did that, I was able to get back on track.

From August 2005 until February 2006, I was walking through a season of confusion and challenge with my boyfriend Malcolm, who is now my husband. We were both stubborn, headstrong, and difficult in our own ways. Every month, without fail, I would break up with him. But somehow, no matter how many times I tried to push him away, he would stay. He would say, "You don't have a good reason for breaking up with me," and sometimes I didn't, but other times, I did. I struggled with what I felt was best for me versus what I knew God was calling me to.

I had to surrender it to God. I told Him, "If Malcolm is the man You've chosen for me, make it work. If not, take him out of my life—but not through death." I realized in that moment that you cannot, and should not, marry anyone who isn't sent by God. If you do, you will live to regret it. I prayed and waited, trusting God's timing, knowing that He would guide me in the right direction.

What I learned through that painful season is this: many of our problems aren't even caused by us. A lot of times, the battles we face come from outside sources—gossip, drama, and people who think they know what's best for us. I would sit back and think of some of the things people said, however it was their opinions and their meddling.

And that's when I realized that silence is often the best weapon. Keep your business to yourself. Don't let others into your relationship, your dreams, or your struggles because people will always have something to say. They'll always try to tear you down. But if you keep things between you and God, no one can destroy what He's building.

During this time, God gave me a vision that would change my life: He placed it on my heart to open a shelter for women in need. I founded my own organization, *Women of the World Reaching Out*. I was determined to have that shelter open by 2007, but just two days after I got married, I lost my job in October 2006.

That was a blow—a huge one. I had worked so hard, and just as I was stepping into a new chapter of my life, the rug was pulled out from under me. But through the pain, I learned this truth: sometimes, God removes something from our lives so He can make room for something greater. He knows what we need even when we don't. And even in the moments of loss, He is still working behind the scenes to fulfill His purpose in us.

My life changed forever. What was once a family of eight is now a family of three. All my brothers are gone, and the pain runs deeper knowing that my sister was found lifeless in another state—far from home. I lost my father, William, a man I admired and looked up to, and my mother, who was on hospice, has also transitioned.

In the midst of this overwhelming grief, I found something I never expected: the grace of God. Through it all, He gave me the strength to keep going, to never give up. He blessed me with the ability to write this book, not just as a story of loss, but as a message of hope, resilience, and faith. I'm here to tell you that no matter how dark the storm gets, if you put God first, He will lead you through. He will guide your steps, open doors you never thought possible, and take you to places you never dreamed of.

Take a moment to look at my journey—half of my life story—and you will see a woman who never gave up. I kept pushing forward, even when the odds were stacked against me. Even when grief threatened to swallow me whole, I held on to God's promises.

I am now a Prophet, and every day of my life, my earnest desire is to please Him and reach out to others—especially young men and women who have walked through the fire, just like I did. I want you to know that you are not alone in your struggles. If you are reading this, know this: No matter what you're facing, you *can* make it. I've been where you are—lost, broken, shattered—and yet here I am, standing firm in Christ.

He brought me from rags to riches, not in material things, but in spiritual wealth, in peace, and in purpose. And He's not done with me yet. There's more—so much more—waiting for you too. So, keep pressing forward. Trust in His timing. Know that even in your deepest sorrow, He is working behind the scenes. And I promise you, if you don't give up, He will take you to a place beyond what you can imagine.

No matter what—*you can make it.*

INSPIRING WORDS

God is the beginning and the end of our lives. He created us, and He knows what will happen in our lives before it even comes. Think about it—God knew you before you were even born. He knows everything we're going through, even before we face it. The things that happen in our lives are meant to make us stronger, so we should count them as blessings, especially when He brings us through them.

But here's where we often go wrong: we start thinking we made it through on our own or that our friends and family helped us. The truth is, they can't save us from our situations—only God can. Too often, we forget to thank Him for the strength to overcome. Instead, we call our friends or family and thank them, but in reality, it's God who brought us through. Remember, if we start giving God the praise and thanks He deserves, our lives will run much smoother.

Another thing we tend to do is put everyone else before God. This could be why many of us find ourselves struggling. We prioritize our spouses, children, or even our parents above God. But do we realize that, just as He gave them to us, He can take them away—just like that? I'm here to encourage you:

examine yourself and ask, "Who is truly first in my life?" Now, I'm not here in front of you, so don't lie to yourself. If God isn't first, it's time to rearrange some priorities.

There were many times in my life when I thought I had God first, but after truly examining myself, I realized I was actually worshiping other things. The Bible tells us in **Matthew 6:33** (KJV), *"But seek ye first the kingdom of God, and his righteousness; and all these things shall be added unto you."* When we put God first and walk in His ways, everything else we desire will fall into place.

THANKS, AND GRATITUDE

First and foremost, I give all glory and thanks to God for giving me the vision and the strength to bring this book to life. Without His guidance, none of this would have been possible. I also want to express my deepest gratitude to my amazing kids, whose unwavering support and encouragement have kept me going through every challenge. To my family, friends, and church family, thank you for believing in me, for pushing me to keep moving forward even when the road felt tough. Your love and prayers have meant the world. God bless you all.